BEACH GAMES FOR KIDS!

Children's Games For Outdoor Fun

In The Sand

by Dan DeFigio

© 2014 Iron Ring Publishing. All rights reserved

No part of this publication or the information it contains may be quoted, reused, transmitted, or reproduced in any form – electronic, mechanical, photocopy, recording, or otherwise – without prior written permission of the copyright holder.

Beach Games For Kids

Table of Contents

Introduction 4

Sharks and Minnows 7

Munchkin Volleyball 9

Angel Faces 10

Water Relay 11

Flying Fish 13

Tic-Tac-Toe 15

Beach Bowling 16

Shell Quest 18

Buried Treasure 19

Super Lungs Ping Pong Race 21

Towel Limbo 23

Sand Darts 25

Dive Under the Ocean 27

Beach Golf 29

About The Author 32

 Pick up a Kindle copy of this book!

www.amazon.com/dp/B00ISWK3PY

If you like this book, please share it on Facebook!

Disclaimer and Terms of Use

Effort has been made to ensure that the information in this book is accurate and complete. However, the author and the publisher do not hold any responsibility for errors, omissions, or interpretation of the subject matter herein, and specifically disclaim any responsibility for the safety or appropriateness of any games presented in this book. This book is presented for entertainment and informational purposes only.

The illustrations in this book were lovingly drawn by Antara Majumder: pixels_graphics@yahoo.com

Introduction

In the summer, families flock to the beaches, and children have the chance to play in a different environment. But after the kids have had their fill of swimming and building sand castles, they sometimes need new ways to have fun while the adults continue to relax!

Beach Games For Kids is a collection of children's games that can be played either with adults for some quality family time, or played by the kids by themselves if the grownups need a little peace and quiet while the kids play.

Safety First!

Any swimming should be done at a lifeguarded area of the beach. Children should always remain within eyesight of an adult. Never turn your back on the ocean, because undercurrents can wash away unwary visitors. Always check the sand in the children's play area for trash or sharp objects, and make sure that any bottles or drinking glasses you bring to the beach are made of plastic so they won't break and leave shards of glass in the sand. Don't forget the sunscreen!

Dynamic Duo Beach Ball Race

What you'll need:

- At least one beach ball (Variation #1 requires more than one ball)

This beach ball game is fun for all ages and is easy to play. Split all the players into teams of two, and give one inflatable beach ball to each team. Draw two parallel lines in the sand approximately 10 yards apart. Each team tries to carry the ball from start line to finish line without touching it with their arms. The ball can be balanced between their heads, pressed between their backs while walking backwards, or set between their stomachs and crab-walked to the end.

Variation #1: Run it as a race, and the first team crossing the finish line wins. For this variation, you'll need one beach ball for each team of two.

Variation #2: Run an elimination game where a team is out if they drop the ball or touch it with their arms. The last remaining team wins.

Variation #3: Use a timer, and the fastest team wins regardless of drops. Remember, you can't use your hands or arms to pick up a dropped ball!

Variation #4: The team that makes the most successful crosses without a drop wins.

Sharks and Minnows

Sharks and Minnows is a great beach game for a large number of kids -- it is most fun with at least 5 players.

Draw two long (at least 20 feet) parallel lines in the sand approximately 10 yards apart. Designate one player to be the Shark (you'll probably get plenty of volunteers!); the rest of the players start as Minnows. Put the Shark in the middle in between the two lines, and line up all the Minnows on one line.

Start the game (you can have the Shark start the game with something like "Yummy, yummy, Minnows for my tummy!")

by having all the Minnows run through the shark tank and across the opposite line. The Shark's job is to tag one (or more) of the Minnows. Any Minnow who gets tagged in the Shark Tank becomes a Shark too, and stays in the tank to help tag the rest of the Minnows. Minnows continue to run back and forth through the shark tank until there is only one Minnow remaining. That player will be crowned the Cleverest Minnow, and gets to start as the Shark for the next game.

Variation: If the players are older and good swimmers, try the game in the water instead of on the sand.

Munchkin Volleyball

Kids love to play volleyball with large beach balls, but standard-sized volleyball nets are too big for small children. You can build a munchkin-sized "net" by making a line of wet sand pylons with a bucket. For a taller net, you can tie a beach towel to the arms of two beach chairs, or you can lay a closed beach umbrella across two beach chairs or two towers built out of sand.

Angel Faces

Have each child lie in the sand and make a sand angel. Have them get out, and draw a face on their Angel. They can make a happy angel, a sad angel, an angry angel, a laughing angel, or any other kind of face you or they can think of. Have each child explain what face they've drawn.

Variation #1: Assign a face for each round. "Everyone make a surprised angel this time!"

Variation #2: Children can draw the faces with their fingers, or they can make faces out of beach debris like shells, seaweed, sticks, or stones.

Water Relay

What you'll need:

- Two small or medium buckets of equal size
- Two plastic drinking glasses of equal size

Beaches are often wide-open spaces that make great places to run. Set up a relay by placing two buckets about 40 yards from the ocean (use a shorter distance for shorter legs). Split up the kids into two teams, and line up each team behind their bucket. When the relay starts, one team member runs to the ocean with a cup, fills it up, and sprints back to the bucket to dump the water into the bucket. The next kid in line grabs the empty cup and makes the same run. The first team to get water to flow over the edge of their bucket wins.

Flying Fish

Draw a wagon wheel shape in the sand – a circle approximately 10 feet in diameter that has lines cut through the center to divide the circle up into eight equal wedges:

One child can volunteer or be selected to be the Octopus, who will stand in the center of the circle and try to capture one of the other children, who will be the Flying Fish.

Each Flying Fish will start in one of the wedges, and when the Octopus yells "Fly!" each Fish jumps into the next counter-clockwise wedge. If any of the Fish fail to land in the next wedge, the Fish will run out of his or her wedge, chased by the Octopus, and run around the outside of the circle until he or she returns to her wedge (like duck-duck-goose). If the Octopus catches the Fish before it gets back to its wedge, the Fish and Octopus change places.

If any Flying fish jumps all the way around the circle before getting caught by the Octopus, the game is over, and the winning Fish will become the Octopus for the next game.

Tip: You'll probably have to redraw the circle and wedges quite often during this game!

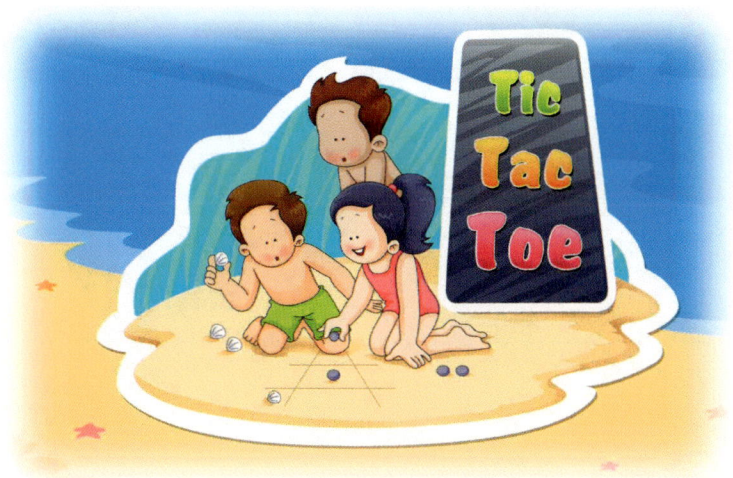

Tic-Tac-Toe

If you're on a rocky beach and drawing X's and O's in the sand is difficult, you can gather rocks and small pieces of driftwood or seashells to use as markers. Divide them out with one player having all the rocks, the other having all the wood or shells. Draw a tic-tac-toe board on the sand, or make one with wood or rocks, and have a Best-of-3 or Best-of-5 tournament.

Beach Bowling

What you'll need:

- 3 tennis balls or baseballs
- Sand shovel or Tablespoon

Dig six shallow holes in the sand in a three-line pyramid (see illustration) – one small (approx. 4" diameter) in front, two medium (6" diameter) in line two, and three large (8" diameter) on the back. Line the kids up behind a line 5 or 10 feet away from the front hole, and have them roll one ball towards the holes. Points are awarding points for sinking a ball into a hole – 1 point for a large hole in the back, 2 points for a medium hole in the middle, and 3 points for the small hole in the front. Each player gets one turn of three rolls, and the one who scores the most points with three balls wins.

Tip: Be sure to use a heavier ball, like a tennis ball or baseball, so it won't blow around in the breeze.

Variation #1: Golf balls will work too, but you'll want to make all the holes half as wide.

Variation #2: Put the roll line on the other side of the pyramid so that the 3-hole line is in front.

Shell Quest

What you'll need:

- A small sand bucket
- Plastic grocery bag, or a large ziplock bag

Collecting shells can be great, especially for younger children. If the beach has enough seashells, you can give a child a quest to collect a bucketful or a bagful of shells. When he or she returns, sit her down and have her sort them by type, by shape, or by color. This is a great quiet-time activity for a smaller child who may be too young to play with the other kids. Children are generally happy with any shell, even broken ones. Celebrate every treasure!

Buried Treasure

What you'll need:

- A time to get down to the beach before the children
- A "treasure" inside a plastic bottle or a box
- One sheet of paper and something to write with

If you can get down to the beach without your children, put some junk jewelry or a special seashell inside a plastic bottle or a box, and bury it under the sand. Draw a treasure map that uses driftwood, rocks, and other landmarks found on the beach. For example, have your map tell the children to "Walk

20 paces" to a log, then turn left. This can be as easy or as hard as you want to make it, and can be great fun for the whole family.

Tip: Be sure to bury your treasure in a place where you can find it later if the kids can't!

Getting Fancy: You can make your treasure map look old by pouring milk on the paper, then letting it dry. After the paper is dry, draw your map in black ink or charcoal pencil. Run a lit match around the edges of the paper to "age" the map.

Variation: If older children need a more challenging game, you can use math in the map directions – the "20 paces" example above could turn into "Walk ye due North with the waves at yer portside, 80 steps divided by 4 be the number before ye turn westward to face the sea."

Super Lungs Ping Pong Race

What you'll need:

- One ping pong ball per child
- Teaspoon or small sand shovel

With a spoon or sand shovel, dig a two- or three-foot diameter circular channel in the sand approximately two inches deep and 1 – 2 inches wide. Have each kid drop the ping pong ball in the channel, and blow it all the way around the circle. No hands allowed! If you blow your ping pong ball out of the trench, you have to start over. Dig as many circles as there are kids, and have a race!

Variation: Use a straight line instead of a circle for smaller lungs.

Towel Limbo

What you'll need:

- One large beach towel

Designate two people to hold the towel as the limbo "stick." When the (optional) music starts, one by one each player bends backwards to pass face-up under the horizontal towel. If you touch the towel or if you fall down, you're out. After everyone has gone once, the towel holders will lower the towel a few inches, and the remaining players will again limbo under one by one. The last player to succeed after everyone else is out wins.

Variation #1: Little kids may have difficulty making it under while bending backwards, so allowing them to go sideways might be a better option.

Variation #2: Have your children play limbo by acting like different sea animals (wiggle like a fish, walk like a crab, flap like a seagull, etc.)

Sand Darts

What you'll need:

- Random toss-able beach debris like rocks, shells, or sticks

Draw a large circle in the sand approximately 6 feet in diameter, with two or three concentric circles inside that one. The players stand behind a line several feet away from the "dartboard" and toss pebbles or shells onto the target, attempting to get as close to the center as possible. Each player gets 5 throws, and the winner is determined by one of these variations:

Variation #1: Count only how many times each player lands one of his 5 "darts" in the center circle. The most center-ring throws wins. Darts in the outer rings can be used to break ties.

Variation #2: Outer ring is 1 point, next ring is 2 points, etc. Count the point total of all 5 darts (good math practice!), and the highest score wins.

Variation #3: The goal is to land one dart in each ring. Keep throwing until you get one dart in the outer ring, then keep throwing until you hit the second ring, etc. After your 5 throws, keep track of your target ring for your next turn. The first player to hit the center (after hitting all the outer rings consecutively) wins.

Dive Under the Ocean

What you'll need:

- Multiple objects of different colors (single-color plastic toys, or seashells that are clearly a particular color)
- A large beach towel or sheet

Dive Under The Ocean is a color-learning game for young children. Put several colored objects under the towel. Call out the child's name and say "(Child's Name), dive under the ocean!" That child goes under the sheet to retrieve an object. When they surface, have them tell you what color it is.

Variation #1: You can send the child Under The Ocean for a particular color ("Dive under the ocean for a BLUE fish!").

Variation #2: You can let the child decide what color he or she will bring up. Ask "Fishy, fishy in the sea, what color fishy will you be?"

Beach Golf

What you'll need:

- Any (safe) throwing object (Frisbee, football, tennis ball, beanbag, etc.)
- One or more targets like a bucket, a rock or piece of driftwood, or a plastic bottle
- A good bit of room on the beach (so no bystanders get hit with thrown objects)

You can use any kind of safe throwing object as the "ball".

Make a 3- or 4-hole course by setting out a number of targets as "holes" at various distances from each other. The goal is to throw the "ball" and get as close to the first "hole" as you can. If you don't hit it the first time, pick up the "ball" and throw it (from where it landed) at the hole again. Count the number of throws it takes to hit the first target, then the next player plays through hole 1. The player who needs the fewest number of total throws to complete the entire course wins.

Tip: If there is a dog on the beach, you'll never get through hole one!

Did you enjoy this book?

Please leave a review – let us know what you liked about

Beach Games For Kids!

www.amazon.com/dp/B00ISWK3PY

About The Author

More books by Dan DeFigio at:

www.amazon.com/-/e/B00CKCEOXA

Dan DeFigio is a recognized exercise and nutrition expert who has been featured on *The Dr. Phil Show*, in *SELF* magazine and *MD News*, on the cover of *Personal Trainer Magazine*, and a number of other publications, television shows, and radio broadcasts.

Since 1993, Dan DeFigio has been on the cutting edge of exercise and nutrition science, leading celebrities, health professionals, and couch potatoes alike down the road to success. His expertise has been shared with thousands of clients and millions of readers worldwide. Dan is the former host of television's Fitness Basics and Beyond, and his most popular book is **Beating Sugar Addiction For Dummies**.

In addition to teaching exercise and nutrition, Dan is a former competitive mixed-martial-arts fighter, culminating his career with a win at the 2000 Pan American Games. Some also say he is quite a piano player.

Printed in Great Britain
by Amazon.co.uk, Ltd.,
Marston Gate.